PROJECT NOTES

Copyright 2014

DATE:

Project:	
Deadline:	
Brief:	

Contacts	Telephone

Items	Actions	✓
		☐
		☐
		☐
		☐
		☐
		☐
		☐
		☐
		☐
		☐
		☐
		☐
		☐
		☐
		☐
		☐
		☐
		☐
		☐

DATE:

Project:	
Deadline:	
Brief:	

Contacts	Telephone

Items	Actions	✓
		☐
		☐
		☐
		☐
		☐
		☐
		☐
		☐
		☐
		☐
		☐
		☐
		☐
		☐
		☐
		☐
		☐
		☐

DATE:

Project:	
Deadline:	
Brief:	

Contacts	Telephone

Items	Actions	✓
		☐
		☐
		☐
		☐
		☐
		☐
		☐
		☐
		☐
		☐
		☐
		☐
		☐
		☐
		☐
		☐
		☐
		☐

DATE:

Project:	
Deadline:	
Brief:	

Contacts	Telephone

Items	Actions	✓
		☐
		☐
		☐
		☐
		☐
		☐
		☐
		☐
		☐
		☐
		☐
		☐
		☐
		☐
		☐
		☐
		☐
		☐

DATE:

Project:	
Deadline:	
Brief:	

Contacts	Telephone

Items	Actions	✓
		☐
		☐
		☐
		☐
		☐
		☐
		☐
		☐
		☐
		☐
		☐
		☐
		☐
		☐
		☐
		☐
		☐
		☐

DATE:

Project:	
Deadline:	
Brief:	

Contacts	Telephone

Items	Actions	✓
		☐
		☐
		☐
		☐
		☐
		☐
		☐
		☐
		☐
		☐
		☐
		☐
		☐
		☐
		☐
		☐
		☐
		☐

DATE:

Project:	
Deadline:	
Brief:	

Contacts	Telephone

Items	Actions	✓
		☐
		☐
		☐
		☐
		☐
		☐
		☐
		☐
		☐
		☐
		☐
		☐
		☐
		☐
		☐
		☐
		☐
		☐

DATE:

Project:	
Deadline:	
Brief:	

Contacts	Telephone

Items	Actions	✓
		☐
		☐
		☐
		☐
		☐
		☐
		☐
		☐
		☐
		☐
		☐
		☐
		☐
		☐
		☐
		☐
		☐
		☐

DATE:

Project:	
Deadline:	
Brief:	

Contacts	Telephone

Items	Actions	✓
		☐
		☐
		☐
		☐
		☐
		☐
		☐
		☐
		☐
		☐
		☐
		☐
		☐
		☐
		☐
		☐
		☐
		☐

DATE:

Project:	
Deadline:	
Brief:	

Contacts	Telephone

Items	Actions	✓
		☐
		☐
		☐
		☐
		☐
		☐
		☐
		☐
		☐
		☐
		☐
		☐
		☐
		☐
		☐
		☐
		☐
		☐

DATE:

Project:	
Deadline:	
Brief:	

Contacts	Telephone

Items	Actions	✓
		☐
		☐
		☐
		☐
		☐
		☐
		☐
		☐
		☐
		☐
		☐
		☐
		☐
		☐
		☐
		☐
		☐
		☐

DATE:

Project:	
Deadline:	
Brief:	

Contacts	Telephone

Items	Actions	✓
		☐
		☐
		☐
		☐
		☐
		☐
		☐
		☐
		☐
		☐
		☐
		☐
		☐
		☐
		☐
		☐
		☐
		☐

DATE:

Project:	
Deadline:	
Brief:	

Contacts	Telephone

Items	Actions	✓
		☐
		☐
		☐
		☐
		☐
		☐
		☐
		☐
		☐
		☐
		☐
		☐
		☐
		☐
		☐
		☐
		☐
		☐
		☐

DATE:

Project:	
Deadline:	
Brief:	

Contacts	Telephone

Items	Actions	✓
		☐
		☐
		☐
		☐
		☐
		☐
		☐
		☐
		☐
		☐
		☐
		☐
		☐
		☐
		☐
		☐
		☐
		☐

DATE:

Project:	
Deadline:	
Brief:	

Contacts	Telephone

Items	Actions	✓
		☐
		☐
		☐
		☐
		☐
		☐
		☐
		☐
		☐
		☐
		☐
		☐
		☐
		☐
		☐
		☐
		☐
		☐

DATE:

Project:
Deadline:
Brief:

Contacts	Telephone

Items	Actions	✓
		☐
		☐
		☐
		☐
		☐
		☐
		☐
		☐
		☐
		☐
		☐
		☐
		☐
		☐
		☐
		☐
		☐
		☐

DATE:

Project:	
Deadline:	
Brief:	

Contacts	Telephone

Items	Actions	✓
		☐
		☐
		☐
		☐
		☐
		☐
		☐
		☐
		☐
		☐
		☐
		☐
		☐
		☐
		☐
		☐
		☐
		☐
		☐

DATE:

Project:	
Deadline:	
Brief:	

Contacts	Telephone

Items	Actions	✓
		☐
		☐
		☐
		☐
		☐
		☐
		☐
		☐
		☐
		☐
		☐
		☐
		☐
		☐
		☐
		☐
		☐
		☐

DATE:

Project:	
Deadline:	
Brief:	

Contacts	Telephone

Items	Actions	✓
		☐
		☐
		☐
		☐
		☐
		☐
		☐
		☐
		☐
		☐
		☐
		☐
		☐
		☐
		☐
		☐
		☐
		☐

DATE:

Project:
Deadline:
Brief:

Contacts	Telephone

Items	Actions	✓
		☐
		☐
		☐
		☐
		☐
		☐
		☐
		☐
		☐
		☐
		☐
		☐
		☐
		☐
		☐
		☐
		☐
		☐
		☐

DATE:

Project:	
Deadline:	
Brief:	

Contacts	Telephone

Items	Actions	✓
		☐
		☐
		☐
		☐
		☐
		☐
		☐
		☐
		☐
		☐
		☐
		☐
		☐
		☐
		☐
		☐
		☐
		☐

DATE:

Project:	
Deadline:	
Brief:	

Contacts	Telephone

Items	Actions	✓
		☐
		☐
		☐
		☐
		☐
		☐
		☐
		☐
		☐
		☐
		☐
		☐
		☐
		☐
		☐
		☐
		☐
		☐

DATE:

Project:	
Deadline:	
Brief:	

Contacts	Telephone

Items	Actions	✓
		☐
		☐
		☐
		☐
		☐
		☐
		☐
		☐
		☐
		☐
		☐
		☐
		☐
		☐
		☐
		☐
		☐
		☐

DATE:

Project:	
Deadline:	
Brief:	

Contacts	Telephone

Items	Actions	✓
		☐
		☐
		☐
		☐
		☐
		☐
		☐
		☐
		☐
		☐
		☐
		☐
		☐
		☐
		☐
		☐
		☐
		☐

Project:
Deadline:
Brief:

Contacts	Telephone

Items	Actions	✓
		☐
		☐
		☐
		☐
		☐
		☐
		☐
		☐
		☐
		☐
		☐
		☐
		☐
		☐
		☐
		☐
		☐
		☐

DATE:

Project:	
Deadline:	
Brief:	

Contacts	Telephone

Items	Actions	✓
		☐
		☐
		☐
		☐
		☐
		☐
		☐
		☐
		☐
		☐
		☐
		☐
		☐
		☐
		☐
		☐
		☐
		☐

DATE:

Project:	
Deadline:	
Brief:	

Contacts	Telephone

Items	Actions	✓
		☐
		☐
		☐
		☐
		☐
		☐
		☐
		☐
		☐
		☐
		☐
		☐
		☐
		☐
		☐
		☐
		☐
		☐

DATE:

Project:	
Deadline:	
Brief:	

Contacts	Telephone

Items	Actions	✓
		☐
		☐
		☐
		☐
		☐
		☐
		☐
		☐
		☐
		☐
		☐
		☐
		☐
		☐
		☐
		☐
		☐
		☐

DATE:

Project:	
Deadline:	
Brief:	

Contacts	Telephone

Items	Actions	✓
		☐
		☐
		☐
		☐
		☐
		☐
		☐
		☐
		☐
		☐
		☐
		☐
		☐
		☐
		☐
		☐
		☐
		☐
		☐

DATE:

Project:	
Deadline:	
Brief:	

Contacts	Telephone

Items	Actions	✓
		☐
		☐
		☐
		☐
		☐
		☐
		☐
		☐
		☐
		☐
		☐
		☐
		☐
		☐
		☐
		☐
		☐
		☐
		☐

DATE:

Project:	
Deadline:	
Brief:	

Contacts	Telephone

Items	Actions	✓
		☐
		☐
		☐
		☐
		☐
		☐
		☐
		☐
		☐
		☐
		☐
		☐
		☐
		☐
		☐
		☐
		☐
		☐
		☐

DATE:

Project:	
Deadline:	
Brief:	

Contacts	Telephone

Items	Actions	✓
		☐
		☐
		☐
		☐
		☐
		☐
		☐
		☐
		☐
		☐
		☐
		☐
		☐
		☐
		☐
		☐
		☐
		☐

DATE:

Project:	
Deadline:	
Brief:	

Contacts	Telephone

Items	Actions	✓
		☐
		☐
		☐
		☐
		☐
		☐
		☐
		☐
		☐
		☐
		☐
		☐
		☐
		☐
		☐
		☐
		☐
		☐

DATE:

Project:	
Deadline:	
Brief:	

Contacts	Telephone

Items	Actions	✓
		☐
		☐
		☐
		☐
		☐
		☐
		☐
		☐
		☐
		☐
		☐
		☐
		☐
		☐
		☐
		☐
		☐
		☐

DATE:

Project:	
Deadline:	
Brief:	

Contacts	Telephone

Items	Actions	✓
		☐
		☐
		☐
		☐
		☐
		☐
		☐
		☐
		☐
		☐
		☐
		☐
		☐
		☐
		☐
		☐
		☐
		☐
		☐

DATE:

Project:
Deadline:
Brief:

Contacts	Telephone

Items	Actions	✓
		☐
		☐
		☐
		☐
		☐
		☐
		☐
		☐
		☐
		☐
		☐
		☐
		☐
		☐
		☐
		☐
		☐
		☐

DATE:

Project:	
Deadline:	
Brief:	

Contacts	Telephone

Items	Actions	✓
		☐
		☐
		☐
		☐
		☐
		☐
		☐
		☐
		☐
		☐
		☐
		☐
		☐
		☐
		☐
		☐
		☐
		☐
		☐

DATE:

Project:	
Deadline:	
Brief:	

Contacts	Telephone

Items	Actions	✓
		☐
		☐
		☐
		☐
		☐
		☐
		☐
		☐
		☐
		☐
		☐
		☐
		☐
		☐
		☐
		☐
		☐
		☐

DATE:

Project:	
Deadline:	
Brief:	

Contacts	Telephone

Items	Actions	✓
		☐
		☐
		☐
		☐
		☐
		☐
		☐
		☐
		☐
		☐
		☐
		☐
		☐
		☐
		☐
		☐
		☐
		☐
		☐

DATE:

Project:	
Deadline:	
Brief:	

Contacts	Telephone

Items	Actions	✓
		☐
		☐
		☐
		☐
		☐
		☐
		☐
		☐
		☐
		☐
		☐
		☐
		☐
		☐
		☐
		☐
		☐
		☐

DATE:

Project:	
Deadline:	
Brief:	

Contacts	Telephone

Items	Actions	✓
		☐
		☐
		☐
		☐
		☐
		☐
		☐
		☐
		☐
		☐
		☐
		☐
		☐
		☐
		☐
		☐
		☐
		☐

DATE:

Project:	
Deadline:	
Brief:	

Contacts	Telephone

Items	Actions	✓
		☐
		☐
		☐
		☐
		☐
		☐
		☐
		☐
		☐
		☐
		☐
		☐
		☐
		☐
		☐
		☐
		☐
		☐

DATE:

Project:	
Deadline:	
Brief:	

Contacts	Telephone

Items	Actions	✓
		☐
		☐
		☐
		☐
		☐
		☐
		☐
		☐
		☐
		☐
		☐
		☐
		☐
		☐
		☐
		☐
		☐
		☐

DATE:

Project:	
Deadline:	
Brief:	

Contacts	Telephone

Items	Actions	✓
		☐
		☐
		☐
		☐
		☐
		☐
		☐
		☐
		☐
		☐
		☐
		☐
		☐
		☐
		☐
		☐
		☐
		☐

DATE:

Project:	
Deadline:	
Brief:	

Contacts	Telephone

Items	Actions	✓
		☐
		☐
		☐
		☐
		☐
		☐
		☐
		☐
		☐
		☐
		☐
		☐
		☐
		☐
		☐
		☐
		☐
		☐

DATE:

Project:
Deadline:
Brief:

Contacts	Telephone

Items	Actions	✓
		☐
		☐
		☐
		☐
		☐
		☐
		☐
		☐
		☐
		☐
		☐
		☐
		☐
		☐
		☐
		☐
		☐
		☐

DATE:

Project:	
Deadline:	
Brief:	

Contacts	Telephone

Items	Actions	✓
		☐
		☐
		☐
		☐
		☐
		☐
		☐
		☐
		☐
		☐
		☐
		☐
		☐
		☐
		☐
		☐
		☐
		☐
		☐

DATE:

Project:	
Deadline:	
Brief:	

Contacts	Telephone

Items	Actions	✓
		☐
		☐
		☐
		☐
		☐
		☐
		☐
		☐
		☐
		☐
		☐
		☐
		☐
		☐
		☐
		☐
		☐

www.ingramcontent.com/pod-product-compliance
Lightning Source LLC
Chambersburg PA
CBHW081909170526
45167CB00007B/3218